CRACKING THE SHELL

THREE KOREAN ECOPOETS

Poems of Seungho Choi,
Chiha Kim, and Hyonjong Chong

Edited and Translated by

Won-Chung Kim

Homa & Sekey Books
Paramus, New Jersey

FIRST AMERICAN EDITION

Copyright © by Seungho Choi, Chiha Kim, Hyonjong Chong
English Translation Copyright © 2006 by Won-Chung Kim

The publication of this book was supported by a grant from
Korea Literature Translation Institute.

All rights reserved. No part of this book may be reproduced,
stored in a retrieval system, or transmitted in any form, or by any
means, electronic, mechanical, photocopying, recording or
otherwise, without prior permission from the publisher.

Library of Congress Cataloging-in-Publication Data

Ch'oe, Sæung-ho, 1954-
Cracking the shell : three Korean ecopoets Seungho Choi, Chiha
Kim, Hyonjong Chong / edited and translated by Won-Chung Kim
—1st American ed.   p. cm.
ISBN 1-931907-40-4 (pbk.)
1. Korean poetry—20th century—Translations into English.
2. Korean poetry—20th century—History and criticism.
3. Ecology in literature. I. Kim, Chiha, 1941- II. Chæong, Hyæon-
jong. III. Kim, Wæon-jung. IV. Title.
PL992.18.S69A235 2006
895.7'108004—dc22   2005019895

Homa & Sekey Books
3rd Floor, North Tower
Mack-Cali Center III
140 E. Ridgewood Avenue
Paramus, NJ 07652

Tel: 201-261-8810; 800-870-HOMA
Fax: 201-261-8890; 201-384-6055
Email: info@homabooks.com
Website: www.homabooks.com

Editor-in-Chief: Shawn X. Ye
Executive editor: Judy Campbell

Printed in U.S.A.
1 3 5 7 9 10 8 6 4 2

Contents

Translator's Note ix
Introduction xi

Part I: Seungho Choi
From the Secular City to the Land beyond Desire

Industrial Complex 3
A Cockroach Family 4
The Pleasures of the Secular City 1 5
The Pleasures of the Secular City 2 6
The Vending Machine 8
In the Refrigerated City 9
Above the Water, Under the Water 10
Bodies 11
Fermentation 12
The Mystery of the Body, or Love 14
Potato 15
The Female Earth 16
Crows 17
The Eyes Flare in Pitch Darkness 18
The Skylark 19
Where Do Sparrows Die? 20
A Butterfly 21
Silkworms 22
A Worm's Words 23
A Snake in the Spring 24
The Slow Walk of the Toad 25
The Death of a Snail in the Woods 26
A Miserable Sow 27
The Eyes of the Shrimp 28
The Lichen 29
If the Sunflower Had Two Arms 30
Cosmos' Flowers 31

The Sound of the Buddhist Temple Bell in Evening 32
The Winter Mountain 33
The Winter Reservoir 34

Part II: Chiha Kim
Heart's Agony for the Cosmic Self

Cracking the Shell 37
  Magnolia 38
  Whatever 39
  In the Past 40
  Heart's Agony 41
  New Spring 3 42
  New Spring 4 43
  New Spring 6 44
  New Spring 8 45
  The Gaps 46
  Respect 47
  Love 48
  Flower-envying Cold 1 49
  Ilsan Poems 2 50
  Ilsan Poem 4 51
  Ilsan Poems 5 52
  Inner Flesh 1 53
  Inner Flesh 3 54
  Nothing 55
  Loneliness 56
  A Memory 57
  Empty Room 58
  My Home 59
  The Sound of Rain 60
  Cricket 61
  Autumn Twilight 62
  A New Church 63
  Late Autumn 65
  The End of a Day 66
  To the West 67

TABLE OF CONTENTS

Part III: Hyonjong Chong
Zenic Correspondence and Ecological Ecstasy

The Dream of Things 1 71
The Island 72
Green Joy 73
A Song in Praise of the Thunder 75
Poetry Writing Class 77
An Elementary School in the Country 79
The Haze of Life 80
To My Nature 81
A Good Landscape 82
The Mystery of the Path 83
After Being Stung by a Bee 85
The Field Is Desolate 86
In a Spoonful of Earth 87
A Flower 88
How Bright It Is! 89
A Song in Praise of Bark 90
In the Spring 92
That Bouquet 93
The Deep Earth 94
A Summer Day 95
The Dew 96
That Curved Line 98
That Toad 99
Trees of the World 100
A God 101
The Sound of Birds 102
My Pleasing Stimulants 103
Flower Petals 105
My Blood Glittering in the Sky at Night 106
The Seeds of Clouds 107

About the Translator

vii

Translator's Note

MY STUDY OF Gary Snyder at the University of Iowa opened my eyes to the beauty and importance of ecological poetry. The fact that traditional Oriental thought was so deeply embedded in Snyder's ecological vision was exciting for me, an Asian student studying English poetry in the U.S. Upon returning to Korea to teach and write about ecological poems, I realized that Korea had its own wealth of ecological poems, though they were not classified "ecological." The translation of Korean ecological poems into English, then, was undertaken in hopes of introducing Korean ecological poems to foreign readers and showing how Oriental thought also influences their writing. This book is, in part, a byproduct of my previous translations of Chiha Kim and Hyonjong Chong. While translating these poets, I found that many of their poems were deeply ecological, which resulted in their inclusion in this new volume. The concern of these poets for the health of this planet called Earth is evident in every corner of their *oeuvre*. They testify that the ecologic problem is not the problem of a single nation but, indeed, that of the whole world. I have decided to translate these three poets because I feel they best represent the different directions Korean ecological poetry is forging.

    I received much help from many people in preparing and publishing this book. I am most grateful to Mijin Kim and James Han, who read the manuscript several times and improved it greatly. Their enthusiasm for the book was indispensable in the completion of this project. Professor Chan J. Wu of Sogang University kindly wrote an introduction to this book and helped me in every phase of translating the work. I appreciate Chiha Kim, Hyonjong Chong and Seungho Choi for kindly allowing me to translate their works. Some of the poems contained in this selection appeared in *Heart's Agony: Selected Poems of Chiha Kim* (White Pine Press, 1998) and *Flowers in the Toi-*

let Bowl: Selected Poems of Choi Seungho (Homa & Sekey Books, 2004). Finally, I must express my deep gratitude to the Korean Literature Translation Institute for their generous funding for the translation and publication of this book. I cannot thank my wife, Hyunsuk, and my children, Lily and John, enough for their unfailing support and care. I give my highest thanks to God, the eternal life-giver and sustainer.

Won-Chung Kim

Introduction

In Search of the Old Future:
The Ecological Imagination of Korean Poetry

Chan. J. Wu

FROM AN ECOLOGICAL point of view, current natural resources do not exist solely for our purposes. Resources are not only the property of our ancestors, but also that of our future generations. Despite this obvious fact, we have been conquering and destroying nature as if it were a commodity we can exploit at will. Therefore, we are face to face with our precarious future. Emerging discourses about ecology, however belated, endeavor to open a new vision of life based on ecological ethics and are quite encouraging. Though the theoretical works of the Deep Ecologists are inspirational and worthy of careful study, it is ecological poetry that appeals more directly to the general public. Ecological poems from all over the world show a fundamental reappraisal and sharp diagnosis of contemporary human civilization, trying to present a viable alternative to the dominant view of nature and human life.

    Korea, in its breathless effort to catch up with the industrialized world, has not been exempt from the exploitation and pollution of nature. In the rapid process of industrialization, Korea's environment has deteriorated and even been mercilessly destroyed. Witnessing such brutal destruction of nature has been very painful for some poets who have been writing ecological, or nature-oriented poetry; it has evoked within them a sense of deep pathos. To address this dire situation, they have exposed and criticized the deterioration of the environment and of human life, while they themselves endeavor to find and present a new vision. This new vision entailed a harmonious relationship between man and nature stemming from the traditional thoughts of the Orient. Of the many poets who have been writing ecologically oriented poems in Korea since the 1970s, Chiha Kim, Hyonjong Chong and Seungho Choi are worthy of special attention. Though their poetic careers, major themes and poetic styles vary, their poems find common ground in their keen explorations of the same ecological devastation and in their attempts to offer solutions. Choi, the youngest of the three, graphically portrays the contaminated environment and its deadly effects on human life; the tension between the destruction and restoration of the integral ecological wholeness captures his imagination. Kim's poems embody the painful reawakening of his mind, from the struggle "with a burning thirst" in the devastated world, to the "sea of life." Lastly, Chong, through his meditation and intuition of Gaia, sings of the ecstasy of life in which man and nature enjoy living harmoniously.

1. Seungho Choi: Criticism of the Culture and Eco-poetics of Disillusionment

With his peculiar poetic spirit and acute observation, Choi critically investigates modern capitalistic civilization. In his poems, the fragments of the dismembered ecological body are grotesquely presented. That these poems appeal to and persuade the reader testifies, paradoxically, that our real world has been led much astray. From a cosmic point of view, he diagnoses human civilization itself as well as the biotic community of the organic earth. Having devoted himself to criticizing the disease of our materialistic civilization, Choi, in his recent works, sings of the broader world of harmony and mutual living. This is an idea he learned from the Buddhistic worldview and the Zenic intuition. He is a poet who perceives the negative and deadly implication inherent in modern civilization as too easily hidden behind the splendid veneer of the secular city. He believes that our environment has been polluted so much that "a brainless

CRACKING THE SHELL

THREE KOREAN ECOPOETS

Poems of Seungho Choi,
Chiha Kim, and Hyonjong Chong

Modern Poetry from Korea
published by Homa & Sekey Books

Flowers in the Toilet Bowl: Selected Poems of Choi Seungho

Drawing Lines: Selected Poems of Moon Dok-su

I Want to Hijack an Airplane: Selected Poems of Kim Seung-hee

What the Spider Said: Poems of Chang Soo Ko

A Love Song for the Earnest: Selected Poems of Shin Kyungrim

Sunrise over the East Sea: Selected Poems of Park Hi-jin

Cracking the Shell: Three Korean Ecopoets
Poems of Seungho Choi, Chiha Kim, and Hyonjong Chong

child" is born from the womb of a woman, caused by no other than man's false and anarchic desire. In a poem titled "Above the Water, Under the Water," tourists "cross the tranquil lake / intoxicated by the beauty / of the surrounding mountains and resort hotels." This means while they enjoy scenes above water, the poet's eye turns downward, below the water, and the ecological wasteland hidden underneath the surface becomes all too visible. Needless to say, it is filled with the wastes of civilization. Human civilization is festering in its poisoned wastewaters and drowning in its own cesspool. The landscape above water, however, is actually even more gruesome and terrible. The frenzy of the fin-de-siècle, ushered forward by the mass insanity, runs rampant everywhere, creating scenes too terrible to watch. There, "a hen, intoxicated, trails her entrails through the night, / though rats gnaw off her breast ("May-Flies at the Dusk")." Furthermore, in the land above water, "the shining flesh of a young harlot / in the red window of the butcher shop" are displayed "at night when the dead fetuses, riding on rusted bikes / run below the red sea, crying for their moms." In short, the world is not much different from the terrible industrial complex:

> After delivering a brainless child,
> the mother felt as if an industrial complex
> had been placed within her body.
> From out of her breasts oozed foamy waste water,
> while a plastic cord dangled from the baby's navel.
> I must have been raped by the smokestacks!
> After birthing her brainless child,
> she wondered if she had nurtured a rubber doll in her
>   womb,
> while plucking out the hair out from her scalp all day
>   long
> to discover whether or not she had a brain of her
>   own.
> ("Industrial Complex")

These words seem too horrible to be uttered in a poem. His comparison of the human body to the industrial complex, in which a belly button and a vinyl rope, and a womb and a rubber doll are paired, is gruesome but accurate. Through these eerie juxtapositions, his assertion that a woman's body—violated by the smokestacks, delivers a brainless child, and white wastewater, not milk, oozes out from her breast—gains credibility. His premonition of the industrial complex's triumph over and modern industry's colonization of the human body, if industrialization continues, is perceptive and convincing. The smokestacks that violate and penetrate the human body are metonymy for the industrial complex located outside our body, but they are, Choi insists, nothing but an outward realization of the limitless desire of our own body.

Choi is a poet who knows all too well that human beings in a capitalistic society, degraded to the position of rats drowning in water, cannot free themselves from the grip of the Mammon. As expressed in the line "Though his body is rather small, his desire was [as big as] dinosaur ("The Dead Man")," excessive desires often drive human beings to their death. Choi rightly points out that these desires are the main causes of the ecological wholeness' destruction. It is true that human beings, acting from these desires, have been exploiting nature and building up their own civilizations. Sadly, when human desires pass their own limits and become anarchic, the desires themselves breed their own desires. He finds that this vicious circle is everywhere, glaring in the frothy and illusory nature of human desires in modern society. In "The Secular City," where the processes of seduction and of being seduced are almost automatic, human beings, like the drowned rat in water, can only move like an automatic doll.

"The Vending Machine" investigates the tragic symptoms of modern civilization as a consumer-oriented society subverting ecological wholeness. The relationship between man and the machine is possible only through money. In such a relationship, any human factor is thoroughly excluded; only the automatic action of the machine, intermediated by money, prevails. Inhuman, automatic life, in which no human feeling can intervene, is expressed through the two images: the prostitute and the money-church. The fall of humankind goes hand in hand with the fall of God. Like the vending machine that provides a pleasing cup of coffee after swallowing money, the prostitute provides momentary pleasure in exchange for money. In this automated money-circuit, the poet identifies the pimp as the most appropriate emblem for fallen human nature. It is he who gathers money in the brothel, the very organization that thrives on the exploitation of helpless women. Churches in the secular city are not much different. The secularized money-church is not willing to bestow blessings on the poor. Instead, it gives "God's orange juice" only to those who have money. In actuality, it is no more than a "vending machine of prostitution" wearing the face of religion.

Choi recognizes the tragic reality of this situation as an illusion that needs to be removed in order to recover true humanity. His poem "The Pleasure of the Secular City 1" attests the paradoxical tragic nature of man's life in an industrialized, capitalist society. There is no limit to the desires of men who are saturated in the illusion, and the consumer-oriented society continuously breeds in them yet another desire that is unrealizable in its very nature. In a world where "the night of capitalism dons a smiles / the leper raises her painted face," man is grotesquely presented as "a chunk of old harlot's meat / hanging in the fresh red-lit butcher's window ("Naked Body")." This illusion continuously exhausts man's life and environment, as well as derails the fundamental grammar of life and death. When the poet says that the life in the secular city is full of pleasure, he is actually criticizing the culture in which man, indulgent in false desires as transient as froth, and the world, promising unlimited pleasure, are enjoying the dance of mutual annihilation. Our imaginations can deduce from his poems that the nightscape of the secular city, staggering in the pleasures of intoxicating desires, must be changed in order to avoid the meaningless dawn of chilling emptiness. This is Choi's characteristic poetics of disillusionment

Choi's poetic strategy of overcoming the illusion changes around the time of *The Reservation of Fireflies*. Up to this point, we have seen him devote himself mainly to depicting concrete, grotesque pictures of illusory desires in *The Pleasure of the Secular City*. In this book of poetry, he, moving past this dismal picture, investigates the intuitive vision of a new world. It is about this time that he shows interest in the Zenic intuition and the Buddhistic wisdom, which teaches the similarities between emptiness and fullness. To use the poet's own words, it was a moment when "the flutter of the heavenly people begins at last, after the long night of alchemy as sore as a gangrene ("Silkworms")." Such a flutter is possible only when one abandons all desires as heavy as dinosaurs and becomes empty and light instead. It is in this context that he emphasizes the pleasure of non-possession in "A Butterfly." But man's life is too heavily burdened with the earthly desires to fly lightly, unlike the birds that soar with the lightness of non-possession. In "The Skylark," Choi laments: "Though I may have two ears as a donkey does, my ears are made to hear only the audible. This is why I hear no messages, even as the tremendous sounds of the universe pierce me like lightening." The poet's correspondence with the sound of the cosmos, and his wish to fly freely and lightly through it, remain as a hope. The moment of poetic sympathy or identification, therefore, is continuously delayed, but this delay adds poetic tension and urges the poet to keep on seeking the new vision for an ecological wholeness.

While watching the cosmos sway in chaos and being unable to live out its own name in an ecologically devastated world, Choi prays in "Cosmos' Flowers" that we might aspire to "a bright world beyond chaos" and reach a cosmic level. This is Choi's vision for the cosmos amid the chaotic reality. In "The Female Earth," this vision is modified, as is his aspiration for the earth, Gaia. Though he moves toward the earth in this poem, the moment of identification with the earth is yet to come. The antagonistic force of the chaos against the cosmos is perhaps too strong to get over at this stage. Nevertheless, the poet's aspiration for a new life is meaningful in itself. In an earlier poem called "The Scraggly Tree of My Soul," he expresses his desire that "someday I can write / poems that have leaves, / poems that yield fruits / and poems that scatter green and gold fragrances." Because he has been looking persistently for an ideal state where ecological wholeness remains untainted, he can hasten his poetic struggle against the anti-ecological reality. The prosaic reality of ecological devastation must have raised strong pathos in the poet who aspired to sing ecological lyrics. This pathos resulted in the grotesque criticism of modern civilization and in Choi's unique poetics of disillusionment.

A little more detailed explanation about Choi's poetic journey toward a new life through disillusionment is needed here. Passing through "The Night of Gangrene," Choi closely approaches the poetic horizon of nothingness. The image of "gangrene" is one that melts away and burns away all things, thereby returning them to their original state of nothingness. Out of the ashes, where no desire can be found, everything aspires to be born again. Out of the gangrenous depths, the "other" and "I" are finally woven together to view the new horizons of mutual living, as Choi writes in "With Your Ash": "Owing to your ash / I become a man who drags the umbilical cord of light." Furthermore, the poet wishes that "my bowels could whisper not to steel wire / but to the overflowing fountains, / and that my dreams could whisper not to the Dead Sea, / but to short grass and cranes and holy souls ("Dough")." In "Fermentation," Choi's wish for a new life is more clearly expressed. The poet sings of his hope that "white reed flowers bloom from beneath the giant film of water and slime / and carps smack and water ducks soar from within that reservoir." He even wishes to feel the breath of fermentation in his own heart. Choi hopes that both the landscape of the wasteland, which the diver notices underwater, and the ecological nightmare above water, witnessed by the woman who delivers a brainless child, can be regenerated anew. To some extent, Choi is an ecologist who writes poems criticizing anti-humanistic and anti-ecological modern civilization. His poems graphically depict the fallen ecological reality and the human desire underlying the devastation. His new vision of ecological harmony and mutual living is based on the Zenic intuition and Buddhistic awakening. In this sense, they can be read as an alternative to the dominant, destructive view held by twentieth-century civilization.

2. Chiha Kim: The Community of Living Things and the Eco-poetics of Full-Emptiness

As it is expressed in the title of his poem "With a Burning Thirst," Chiha Kim was a poet who has endured and fought deadly reality and extreme agony. He has experienced various kinds of persecution, has been at the threshold of death and has been caught in the vortex of industrialization and military dictatorship. On the other hand, in the center of persecution and burning thirst, he paradoxically found a true "sea of life" that helped him overcome a death-infested reality. The dialectic tension and conflict between the anti-democratic reality and his yearning for democracy constitutes the main tenor of his early poems. Gradually, his poetic vision develops into a profound ecological vision of the solidarity of all living things, comprised of man and man, man and nature, and man and cosmos. This is a world of nirvana where the distinction between life and death is broken down completely. In this new and open world, every creature helps the other to fully realize life by freely supporting, embracing and interpenetrating each other. In short, this world is a "full-empty" universe, a perfectly rounded world of harmony between fullness and emptiness.

Kim was imprisoned as a means of political retaliation against his poems that parodied existing political corruption. Instead of finding indignation in prison, he found the true meaning of life. By synthesizing and reinterpreting Korea's traditional folklore and Tonghak thought, he created a new paradigm that allowed him to leap over the conflicting duality of the world. This new paradigm of life resulted from his having experienced the extremities of life and death. He diagnoses the present as the age when every life is being destroyed daily. Explaining that life is a key word in leading the people to recognize the importance of the problem, Kim argues for the urgency of recovering the essential nature of life, which is boundless, free, creative and dynamic as it creates harmony.

While Kim expresses his sympathy and love for all creation in *Aerin*, he sings of rebirth and new life in *Heart's Agony*. This is a noteworthy change, one that demonstrates Kim's ever-continuing insight into his own life and literature as he journeys through life. Here, the mature poet, in his earnest desire to become a cosmic self, investigates the principle of circulation and mutual living through which the reverse reaction of the cosmos is possible. As it is expressed in the lines "I hear / The rain / Which falls from the sky and / Soars on back, after traveling to the earth" ("The Sound of Rain") or in "Within a drop of contaminated water / I am imprisoned // Thus closed / I am born again // I wriggle // I dream of / Blue sky and white cloud / Over the mountain" ("Reversal"), life and death, descent and ascent, closeness and openness are not separate entities but organically connected in the poet's imagination. Kim's marvelous vision of a new life in which he deconstructs all distinction, subverts all positions and widens all gaps so that all living entities can interpenetrate one another is not much different from the cosmic principle of mutual living through transformation; "Cracking the Shell" is one of his best poems embodying this idea:

> At evening,
> A green star burns
> In my loins.
> It rises above my navel
> Into my skull.

I am burnt hollow,
And now a tree grows in me.
Dead and transformed
Into a crescent moon,
I rise over the trees.

Love,
Let me know
The mystic hour of birth.

I'll break my shell
Kicking through
To be born again
Like the Universe.

The second stanza of the poem demands special attention. This stanza expresses Kim's intuition of the organic principle of the circulation of the body, fire, ash, tree and moon. It also tells us that life is imperishable and that this eternal life permeates our body. Terms such as "new birth," "love" and "born again" indicate that Kim is pursuing a life in which the cosmic principle is fully actualized based on the realization of the interconnectedness of every living thing. This is, indeed, a significant change for Kim who once encouraged the spirit to revolt against deadly reality. In his persistent pursuit of the principle of new life based on the interconnectedness of living things, he can sing that "Out of the bottom of despair / The cosmos emerges ("New Spring 7")." Because "Love / Cosmic and unknown / Shoots out like wind / From my empty heart ("Nothing")," the poet can sing "My heart leaps / At the wonder of all living things ("New Spring 6")." Having experienced this love, the poet can clearly see "The bud of the cosmos / Shoots everywhere ("Respect")."

The landscape of this new life beyond the death-infected present is similar to the sea of Buddha, where cosmic buds shoot out and every living thing helps the other, thereby attaining a state of harmony. The poet, who is singing in this sea of life "the song of myself / Born anew within my old self," is a shaman of the full-empty universe. The shaman presents to the world great affirmation by humiliating himself before and showing respect to the cosmic force of life. Kim's later poetry, born of a weary body and soul that experienced repression, imprisonment, and sickness, is comparable to a cosmic tree that never stops sending out new shoots. Needless to say, ecological imagination plays an essential role in shaping this song of cosmic buds.

In Kim's poetic career, the transition from the political imagination to the ecological imagination is prominent. While the former relies heavily on a worldview of binary oppositions, the latter stems from the view of a cyclical universe. His political imagination shows a strong pathos of confrontation, revolt, criticism and satire. His ecological imagination is one of compassion, interconnectedness, love, embrace, respect and transformation. This shift is representative of the change in thought within Korean society in the latter half of the twentieth century and accords with the present worldwide concern for nature.

3. Hyonjong Chong: Meditation of Gaia and the Eco-poetics of Ecstasy

Hyonjong Chong is a poet who breathes the language of trees. His heart is open to the universe, and his words are airy breezes that plant cosmic trees in a sick world. He is an innocent dreamer who dreams a nirvana out of agonizing reality. To him, his life, breath and poetry are inseparable; he lives as he dreams and creates poetry with the breath of dreams. In this dreamy texture, all life in this world falls into ecstasy unaware. The fact that he falls into ecstasy just as he falls into dreams does not necessarily mean that his life in this world has been easy. On the contrary, dreaming is often the antithesis of harsh reality. Having the marvelous skill of transforming agony into celebration and misery into happiness, Chong never gives up dreaming of free flight, or of the ecstasy of life even in the vortex of painful and life-destroying reality. He shows the metaphysical depth of vision in his pursuit of the intimate correspondence between the self and the poetic objects, and in his effort to grasp the ultimate meaning of life with his free poetic spirit. His poetic world, where he sings of life's ecstasy perceived through Zenic intuition, is certain to be one of the highest peaks of Oriental spiritualism.

    The burden of existence makes the poet's life almost unbearable. Corrupt power is destined to warp a man's life. The vitality of life is castrated and the energy of the soul is weakened. Man is in danger of losing even his capacity to laugh, which helps him endure his painful reality. Taking full advantage of this situation, the brazen capitalism of materialistic society ruthlessly destroys nature, home of all living things. The poet's ominous statement in "The Field is Desolate" reflects the effects of such contamination of nature. The poet is standing in the golden autumn field of ripening rice, where the air used to be endlessly filled with the noisy sound of grasshoppers' wings. Now the field is, indeed, desolate. With the excessive spraying of agricultural chemicals, the chain-link of grasshoppers in the circle of life has been broken. We can easily imagine where the poet's lamentation, "Oh, this ominous silence—/ the golden chain of life is broken," originates. At this moment, the antenna of the poet becomes hypersensitive to the living things around him. This is none other than an example of Chong's struggle to recover the original self, warped and crushed by a culture that threatens life, and his attempt to make room for a freer, life-giving breath.

    In "Exclamation Mark," Chong's struggle expresses itself as an action of putting exclamation marks on all the living things of nature such as trees, flowers and bird songs. Though the poet's sense of humor is apparent in this poem, what takes utmost importance is his desire to be one with nature through innocent feelings. The desire to be one with nature is well expressed in the lines "every moment / is a flower bud / which will bloom / with my enthusiasm ("Every Moment is a Flower Bud")." In order to enjoy this moment when these flower buds bloom, Chong eagerly communicates with and penetrates into "the other" that includes nature. The poet resuscitates the breath of life by identifying himself with nature, something that attracts him irresistibly. The vigorous energy of life, as expressed in the words "I come to return to my nature / unaware // What exuberance overflows the levees!" can characteristically be found in the universe of Chong's "Poetry Writing Class"; the energy is followed by the world of green joy and ecstatic life. Chong's poetic sensitivity, which finds a cosmic joy in green leaves, can be easily found in many poems including "Green Joy." Sharing the poet's perspective that intuits the principle of the whole universe in things as seemingly insignificant as a blade of grass, readers will find themselves intoxicated by the fragrance emanating from "the Sky [which] is itself / all joy and a shrine." When we follow the dynamic movement of creation as perceived by Chong, we, too, are poets. The poet's desire to be lost in the ecstasy of life, however, stems from the worsening state of life-threatening reality. Chong's poetry is, in an important sense, his reaction to, and criticism of, capitalistic civilization, the violent nature of materialist society and the anthropocentric hubris of man.

In his *Gaia*, J. E. Lovelock explains that Gaia is a biosphere, an organism with the capacity to keep the earth healthy through autonomous control of the physical and chemical environment. Taking this view of Gaia, one realizes that there is no difference between humankind and microorganisms; they are equal because both perform their roles on this planet and have their own value as organisms. Because Chong is a poet who meditates about man and the biosphere from Gaia's point of view, his poetry beautifully embodies the spirit of Gaia. While "In a Spoonful of Earth" clearly expresses the poet's perception of the Gaia phenomena and his recognition of mystery and ecstasy, "A Good Landscape" opens a new horizon in his meditation of Gaia by delicately capturing the intense sensual joy. With the blessings of nature symbolized by the mellow snow, the couple makes love against a chestnut tree in the woods. In a strict moral sense, this scene may seem a bit crude. Yet the poet encompasses this act as an essential element of nature within his view of "a good landscape," in exemplifying poignantly the beautiful harmony between man and nature. His colorful observation that the woods have contributed to the couple's intense lovemaking, and that their lovemaking has stimulated the early blossom of the chestnut tree, comes from Chong's perceptive intuition of the original interconnected order of man and nature. This order is harmonious and circular, as well as mutually supportive of each other. The poem serves as a good example showing us the fruit of Chong's meditation on Gaia, and the depth and ecstasy of life.

Chong's dream, based on his meditation of Gaia, follows the breaths of life and the original blueprint of the cosmic spirit. The ecological spirit that tries to recover and praise the beauty of all life and is rapidly disappearing from today's materialistic civilization, permeates his poetry like a myth. Chong, "a cosmic child," to use Gaston Bachelard's term, feels the beautiful breath, the pleasing stimulation of all living things and the phenomena of their living. When the poet sings, "I will trust my body to my pleasing stimulants; / thunder and lightening / birds of the world / trees of the earth / flowers and grass / pretty women / full moons about to burst / shudder! Insects / those terrible animals and / your / fragrant breath ("My Pleasing Stimulants")," we can easily spot the burgeoning of his poetic spirit.

These "pleasing stimulants" are the important "others" in Chong's poetry. As stated before, his poems are created through the process of reaching for, and penetrating into, these "others." He writes poems of high density that capture dynamic moments of correspondence in which his unconditional creative self-abandonment or the absolute freedom of poetic self are fully realized. To reach this moment resembling that of

INTRODUCTION

Zenic awakening, Chong intentionally escapes the tunnel of daily life and looks to the source of nature's splendid light.

In this splendid light, the universe of "the expanding, throbbing heart" changes into "a karaoke bar" ("A Tiger on My Shoulder"), as if in a dream. Naturally, all things look different. "Trees of the World," full of life's energy, grow and soar into cosmic trees:

> I wonder what kinds of works
> trees of the world are doing?
> They willingly take root in the soil of the man
> who enjoys watching them.
>
> Day after day he watches them and loves them more
> until his heart pounds wild and blue at their beauty.
> They push up saps in every corner of the body
> and channel their saps higher and higher up to the sky.
> They are springs of perfect-round tension!
>
> Trees! Don't you hear day after day
> the ever-expanding, throbbing energy of first love
> full in the sky, on the earth, and in our hearts?
> ("Trees of the World")

The trees in Chong's poem are brimming with life's energy. These cosmic trees connect not only the sky and the earth, but also the energy of people, making all things dance with the joy of living. With the trees' rising and expanding motion, the heart of the universe throbs like the lovers' hearts upon first love. This tree image is a development from Chong's early image of the wind that stood for his wish to soar. This forest of trees, love and life is, indeed, sufficient to afford the weary soul rest and peace. Furthermore, hearing the beat of birds' wings will double the joy. Intoxicated by the harmony of the trees and birds in the forest, Chong at last resuscitates the previously-lost circular memory of the cosmic spirit.

The infinite ways poetry branches into the universe weaves into a deep, freely moving and mysterious breath in "The Dew." The circular shift and movement—from tree to cloud, to river, to bird and to sky—stems from his circular memory, connected to the myth's archeology. This circular memory is the basis of his perception of eternal flux and transformation. Eternal flux is simple but filled with innocence, like the music of Bach. In this sense, Chong's poetry is a dream, a longing for the innocence of the soul.

Chong's desire to be like a bird reflects his view of the human condition; birds serve as a concrete object with the freedom of flight that intimidates man who is bound to earth. Without soaring, how is it possible to recover our circular memory? Nietzsche's philosophy of lightness and Bachelard's theory of imagination are also associated with the imagery of birds. Birds give us an opportunity to reflect on our lives in this world. They awaken in us the importance of pulling back from the modern way of life, imposed on us by modernization. Chong emphasizes the urgency of recovering the original way of cosmic order and nature, which he believes is the natural path our lives should follow. Therefore, what matters most is our endeavor to recover our lost memory of the universal circularity, most apparent in "O": "O is a beginning and an end. / O is the portrait of life. / O is a shape which has everything as well as nothing in it, / full and empty at the same time." O is also "the breath of life" and "the mirror of life / O is love."

Chong intuits a poetic vision on the universe's grand order by reflecting it in this "mirror of life." He is a poet who wishes to breathe fresh and freely into, and with, the universe to open the pathways polluted by our daily lives. To help us breathe more easily, he lets his voice ring, singing ecstatically from the depths of his wisdom and resuscitating our lost memory of the universe's circularity. His readers, then, may touch the circular

INTRODUCTION

fabric of his *oeuvre*, his archeology of myth, and finally enter happiness.

Chan. J. Wu
Literary Critic / Professor of Korean Literature
Sogang University
Korea

(Translated by Won-Chung Kim)

Part I: Seungho Choi
From the Secular City to the Land beyond Desire

PART I: SEUNGHO CHOI

Industrial Complex

After birthing a brainless child,
the mother felt as if an industrial complex
had been placed within her body.
From out of her breasts oozed foamy waste water,
while a plastic cord dangled from the baby's navel.
I must have been raped by the smokestacks!
After birthing her brainless child,
she wondered if she had nurtured a rubber doll in her womb,
while plucking out the hair out from her scalp all day long
to discover whether or not she had a brain of her own.

A Cockroach Family

In the vending machine that always
consumes and satisfies the desire of the consumers,
there lives a cockroach family.
Their appearances are shiny.
like a pimp's family living off the whores.
The brothel's morning
begins when the hole swallows the money.
The smell of coffee and milk is warm,
and the sugar and dreams are limitless.
With the falling sound of the last coin,
night comes, but the stillness of night
is ruptured by night's sleepless desire.
A cockroach family lives in the vending machine
whose rubber hose, connected to the water container,
like a whore's urethra is connected to the urinary bladder,
pours hot water into paper cups.
Our limit to love is the same
as that of this small, tight-knit family.

PART I: SEUNGHO CHOI

The Pleasures of the Secular City 1

A girl double
does the sex scene
far too graphic for the star actress.
Cast onto the silver screen,
she's as naked as a skinned chicken.
She sells her faceless body,
flinging her carnal lust about.

In the darkness of the theater
I sit as a spectator.
Lust begins to bulge with illusion,
and the illusion arouses excitement within.
I know, of course, that the images passing before my eyes
are merely the reeling of a fragmented film,
a flickering of nothing more than an illusion.
Still, I watch, intoxicated by the illusion,
the live unfurling of the illusion to its very end,
until the screen of my pupils goes blank,
and the tongue protruding from my eyes hangs dead.

CRACKING THE SHELL

The Pleasures of the Secular City 2*

The woman who had been moaning bitterly,
a money belt around her mourning dress,
checks her profits and losses late at night.

The cold storage room is now hushed.
There lie the empty, open hands of the penniless person,
bereft of all the things he had taken pains to gather.
(Great woe to the great thief!)
The man, finally unburdened through death,
lies naked in cold storage.

The flower cards players, roving their coin-sized eyeballs, are
    in agony about
whether to play the black-clover or red-clover card.
Even on this night of death, they chuckle
and are drunk in the pleasure of winning small change.

An all-night vigil for the lonely body.
The King of the Dead, holding a smelly toothpick,
peeps into the night as the mice grind their teeth,
hesitating between the silence and the grain of memory
that will soon become chaff.

The cold storage room is silent.
On this night when the naked body, placed within a thin straw
    mat,
lies in a tongue-frozen cold,
a mortician, holding the cloth of the next world in his hand,

PART I: SEUNGHO CHOI

comes in and places his ear to the mouth of the body
as if to ask to whom he should now pose questions of death.

An emptiness
too frigid
even for the dead body to emit.

---

* It is customary in Korea for mourners to bring money to the bereaved family and to keep an all-night vigil.

CRACKING THE SHELL

The Vending Machine

Orange juice was what I wanted
but I pushed the button for coffee instead.
This is the danger of a habit.

A horrible habit drags me along
like a hypnotist who
takes me as a somnambulist,
into the foggy country of custom and routine.

I have to come to my senses, I mutter.
I drink the unexpected coffee
to take hold of myself, to clear the dense fog
within my head, dulled from fixed ways.

The vending machine is, to me, a prostitute,
whose eyes light up and become turned on
the moment a coin is offered.
It is a money church.
Who is the pimp who rakes its money?
If you already know the power of money
then you know too well you need only insert it
and the vending machine whore
will service you with a cup of her saccharin pleasure.
I wonder if the vending machine, the one with the cross on it,
will be able to supply God's orange juice?

PART I: SEUNGHO CHOI

In the Refrigerated City

On a summer day, when the whales
pierced by the harpoons of whaling ships
twist and spout blood into the sea,
goods are displayed under a cold current of air in the super-
    market.
The surveillance camera above my head
and the mirrors here and there watch me,
and the small crabs, refusing to be ransomed,
swarm and give off foam from the sea.

The small crabs in the huge barrel
are dying.
The cold currents flow silently
amongst the shriveled onions,
shoals of anchovy,
and the cleaned green onions and crowned daisies;
my consciousness touches
the cold bone of the dead fish in the refrigerator.

The supermarket downtown,
where women, holding shopping baskets,
peep and meander between the goods and the labels,
sails like a merchant ship in a summer of noise and sun.
In the bone the warm blood begins to circulate
and the cosmic current of blood swirls.

Above the Water, Under the Water

When the tourists cross the tranquil lake

divers plunge down to its bottom
to haul up the dead body,
but at the bottom they see a huge mound of waste,
a belly that's bloated and silently growing bigger,
a giant waste mound filled with:
abandoned shoes, broken plastic containers, pieces of vinyl,
all wallowing in a muddy water and silt
in which the deserted fetuses and larvae of cats and dogs lie
    mangled.
The mound swells bigger and bigger
like that of a cadaver.
The divers observe sullen pond snails whose bowels rot, poi-
    soned by toxins,
and the evidence of decaying civilizations that originated near
    the water,
rotting away from untreated sewage being excreted from pipes

while the tourists cross the tranquil lake,
intoxicated by the beauty
of the surrounding mountains and resort hotels.

PART I: SEUNGHO CHOI

Bodies

Oh God, groaning in pain
you are to be pitied above all others.
Only when we cease to be a cancerous mass
can Your body be sound.

The crimson lust of the tongue, our whole bodies thus concentrated,
swirls back and forth vigorously
swelling like a bloated cluster of maggots.

Fermentation

I am trying to ferment
this rotting reservoir in my heart.

I have decayed enough while living;
old bureaucrats have dumped hardened stool on me
and I, a meek, lowly person,
have accepted their disgrace as mine.
Who in this land is free of stench?
When the bruised face was rotting at the bottom of the lake
or when it floated up to the surface of the turbid water,
I kept silent
and accepted the sorrow as mine.
As a man who should have died long ago
or a man whose gall had become blackened by a poisonous
      age,
I merely foamed at the mouth instead of shouting out bitterly.
But the problem was that the more I struggled against the waste,
closing the lid of my mind, the more waste was produced.
I found out too late that the lid was but a coarse mesh net.

A Mulwang Reservoir sign is posted along a border in my mind.
I have never seen the reservoir in person.
I have only glanced at the signpost of the Mulwang reservoir
through the window of a dusty bus, on a drought stricken day.
I pray that
the law of the water, the way of Mulwang
still operates within the reservoir.
And I hope that the water snakes seeping through the sedge

are alive like a dance in that place.

I also pray

white reed flowers bloom from beneath the giant film of water
and slime

and carps smack and water ducks soar from within that reservoir,

and that as the breath of fermentation moves about powerfully
my mind shares in its vitality.

The Mystery of the Body, or Love

The body stitches
the hands' open wounds.
Whether wide awake
or fast asleep
or enveloped in dreams of false images,
the body has been stitching for more than a fortnight.
The body seems to love its hands,
and seems unashamed of
the hands attached to it.

These begging hands, these stealing hands,
these hands that snatch things
as the fingers grow outstretched,
but that clench into fists of hatred when things are taken away,
these hands, whose fingernails grow till they curve,
that play with pubic hair and shake the hands of adultery,
and the hands that pray for blessings
from the grotesque, decayed idols of a thousand years ago—
the body seems unashamed of
these dirty hands that are attached to it.

The body stitches with ease
the hands' open wounds.
Though neither the golden needle nor the golden thread is seen
the body stitches the wound tight all day and night.

Oh, the mystery of this body
or love!

PART I: SEUNGHO CHOI

Potato

After our bare bodies are pushed out of the womb, we wander about dirt and asphalt roads and concrete stairs and grow older without knowing who we are. At last when we turn our eyes that have looked outward within, to illuminate our insides, we acknowledge that nothing of ours is actually ours, and notice the empty field that existed before birth, and then potatoes will roll toward us as a giant blessing and present themselves on our dinner table. All food is sacred in that it sacrifices itself. All tables are, therefore, feasts. Even the merest of morsels.

The Female Earth

Carrots, radishes, and potatoes are born of the earth, aren't they all? Pine nuts, wild vines, and red elderberries thrust their roots deep into the earth and stand strong, don't they? The fruits that ripen in clusters under the autumn sky are now returning to their homes, like a salmon returning to its mother stream to spawn. By dying into the female earth, they hope their offspring will prosper ever after.

Crows

As if the pitch-black energy of the night were within them, their bodies are possessed of luster and tautness. And even though their voices are coarse, without a doubt they are heaven's singers. On days when these black birds take flight, the sun is certain to shine brighter.

The Eyes Flare in Pitch Darkness

A little after midnight the power went out. I opened my door looking outside to see if it was my house only or the whole village that was out of electricity. Great things have no shape, so the proverb goes, and so the whole universe had become shapeless. My eyes flared and my mind grew enlightened, and I could hear the sound of the stream flowing endlessly through the darkness.

PART I: SEUNGHO CHOI

The Skylark

Against a soundless blue sky, a skylark dons the sun as its halo and breaks into song, creating a golden ripple in the barley field. The barley is without ears, but I wonder if it grows as it listens to the skylark's song ascending into the sky. Though I may have two ears as a donkey does, my ears are made to hear only the audible. Which is why I hear no messages, even as the tremendous sounds of the universe pierce me like lightning.

Where Do Sparrows Die?

A sparrow lies dead on a mound of snow between the clay jars on the terrace. Though impossible to know whether it died of hunger or from the frost, or from the poisoning of fertilizer chemicals, a sparrow that is dead means that it is warm no longer. Being dead means that it flies no longer. Being dead means that it twitters no longer. I hold the sparrow, and its body is stiff and cold as a lump of ice. Was this one of the sparrows that would fly to the dog's food bowl, with begging eyes and bobbing tail to peck at the tips of the yellow bean sprouts? Sparrows die in the small spaces between jars. They also die under cherry trees and at the feet of scarecrows. Sparrows are meant to die on the earth. The entire earth is their grave. After all, there is no place in the sky where you can bury anything — not even a feather.

A Butterfly

I have never seen a butterfly bear a load on his back or haul freight with a rope as a helicopter does. All he has is his light body, and this body is all he possesses. Nothing can ever bind him. With the lightness of non-possession, he flies freely. Flowers are his watering holes, and leaves, his shelter from the rain. His life amounts to a fluttering dance, and only death can stop his rhythm. In his old age, dying away, he wants for nothing. Because he desires nothing, even when dying, he is free.

Silkworms

Silkworms are hermits. They enter into a white cave of their making, close the doors and quietly hide themselves away. During the time of huddling in solitude the transformation of their beings takes place. Cells are arranged all anew and wings that had never been, come into creation. Would this mysterious metamorphosis have been at all possible without the power of a dream? One day fresh morning faces will emerge from the caves. Only after long nights of alchemy, as painful as the suffering of gangrene, can the fluttering of heavenly people begin. There is no king of the silkworms who creates a hole for escape from outside the caves. For silkworms know all too well that they must tunnel their holes on their own, and that the hole must lead outward from deep within.

PART I: SEUNGHO CHOI

A Worm's Words

Having no eyes, I adored no idols. Having no arms, I reached out to no one. And because the struggle of daily survival was enough, I chose sleep over penance.

A Snake in the Spring

A snake in the spring is not to be loathed. Far from loathsome, it is to be pitied instead. I watched a feeble, haggard snake coming out of its burrow. And I wished that the frogs would come out early from their hibernation so that the snake could be enticed to garner its strength. Whether I should save the snake or spare the frog is my own personal dilemma. At times, I'll have the snake disgorge the frog by pressing its throat with my pole, and at others I simply let the snake be and allow it to swallow the frog or field mouse.

Unlike an autumn snake whose scales are glossy with venom, a snake in spring lacks vigor and slithers along lifelessly. Burdened by a fate to never lift its belly from the ground, and a sorrowful search for food to survive, the spring snake moves listless and alone through a stony field with no path.

PART I: SEUNGHO CHOI

The Slow Walk of the Toad

These fellows saunter about slowly. Waddling and toddling, their four legs push off the ground leisurely two by two, like the movement of the legs of a student's desk maneuvered. I have seen them by a lonely hermitage in the deep mountains. When still, they have the look of solemn and austere meditators, and when moving, the look of a gentlemen. Were it not for an untrodden mountain path with moss-covered rocks, such a slow walk and disregard for the ways of the outside world would be impossible. While such a thing will surely never happen, but were they ever to walk across the asphalt road that lies at the foot of the mountain, their bodies would be crushed like smeared jelly or tofu. And many people would grieve the tragedy.

The Death of a Snail in the Woods

Here lies a dead snail without even its shell. On the woodland path, upon which the yellowish pine needles fall, its naked body, the size of a little finger, lies prostrate. No longer does it move, grope with its round, black tentacles, nibble plants in the night, nor dribble its sticky saliva. It waits only for the hour of decay, discarded alone in the woods, where the trees light no lamps for its funeral. It is a death without even a shell, a death that has nothing more to offer but its own naked body.

PART I: SEUNGHO CHOI

A Miserable Sow

One day a sow, while feeding eight piglets she had just delivered, suddenly bit them to death as if she were mad. At first, the farmer was saddened by this incomprehensible, enormous event, but later, he became indignant. Considering the amount of money the eight piglets would have brought him, and that this money had now been turned into manure by the sow's riotous act, his indignation was understandable. Nevertheless, it was not necessary to kill the sow. But the farmer cut her throat himself. A really angry man is little different from a madman. One should beware madness. It was later said that a long nail had been found in her molar. Being a dumb animal, the irritation and pain would have been even greater. Later, at a neighborhood meeting, the villagers promised not to put steel pieces such as crooked nails and needles in the food trough anymore. But the farmer, holding the miserable sow's head in his bosom, wept bitterly for her and for his own foolish behavior, which he could not undo even by cutting his own throat.

The Eyes of the Shrimp

By the lakeshore one night, I shone a flashlight into the water and saw the eyes of a fresh-water shrimp coming toward me, its two protruding eyes gleaming like gold. I remember those eyes, two yellow beads at the bottom of the lake, to be more beautiful than the clearest eyes I had ever seen. I wonder if it would not also be beautiful to leave the memory of those lovely eyes alone by the lake with the moon rising, rather than spoil them by trying to capture them with my words.

PART I: SEUNGHO CHOI

The Lichen

There are rocks over a thousand years old that still do not know how to coax open a flower. Meanwhile, there is moss that, although living only a year, knows how to put tiny red flowers no larger than dust into bloom. If you look carefully, you can see tiny busy flies, fluttering and crowded, within these flowers.

If the Sunflower Had Two Arms

The sun shines overhead, but the lanky sunflower has fallen low to the ground. If the sunflower had two arms, however short, maybe it would not lie collapsed as it does as if to bury its face into the earth. The face of the sunflower lying on its side; Buddha himself assumed such a posture when he entered nirvana. Nirvana on the road. Death on the road, where we are from and where we return in the end. But the sunflower insists on a life in one spot, and lives as if to bury its old face under its roots, with its back against the long, summer sun.

PART I: SEUNGHO CHOI

Cosmos' Flowers

Cosmos flowers cluster along the dark asphalt road. Whenever trucks pass they seem to tumble to the earth, but they simply sway and then rise again erect. Pair of lovers walk leisurely along that cosmos blossom road. *Yin* and *Yang*, arms linked affectionately, approaching in cosmic steps, not into the original chaos but into the bright world, toward the universe.

The Sound of the Buddhist Temple Bell in Evening

While walking along a path in the woods, where the wind had hushed, I unexpectedly heard the sound of a temple bell. This sound reminded me that the Original Mind, which grows fainter as life proceeds, was still unfurled in me like a blue sky in mud. And I wondered if I alone had remained a dull blockhead, while the bamboo and oak trees had already awakened, poised and calm. If I am, in truth, the lone blockhead in the universe, the sound of this bell must be ringing again and again to crack no one but me — a man as dull as an iron ball.

PART I: SEUNGHO CHOI

The Winter Mountain

The winter mountain is a hotel without beds. The frogs, snakes, and squirrels check in as long-term guests and sleep throughout the entire winter. Curled up with their heads buried in their bellies, they all wait for spring. They will endure the winter like nestled eggs.

The winter mountain is a hotel without blankets. Without blankets, the creatures need lots of fur to survive, but frogs and snakes do not have a single tuft. They are forced to endure the long winter bare.

The winter mountain is a hotel without lights. Creatures with their mouths frozen hard as stones endure the winter in darkness.

.

The Winter Reservoir

The reservoir froze over with last night's cold. It froze so hard, a huge sheet of plate glass, not a crack could be found for the ducks to dip their bills in. It is too silent. I throw a stone the size of my fist into the heart of the cold stillness. A banging sound, and then the stone sliding toward the middle of the lake as if riding on a sled. It stops, and then begins to freeze into the stillness. The fish underneath must have heard the bang, and been stirred into moving their fins. But that was not my intent when I threw the stone. The dawn of creation begins with the breaking of silence.

Part II: Chiha Kim
Heart's Agony for the Cosmic Self

PART II: CHIHA KIM

Cracking the Shell

At evening in my body,
A green star burns
In my loins.
It rises above the navel
Into my skull as well

I'm burnt hollow,
And now a tree grows in me.
Dead and transformed
Into a crescent moon,
I rise over the trees.

Love
Let me know
The mystic hour of birth.

I'll break my lining
Kicking through
To be born again
Like the Universe.

Magnolia

When I open my eyes,
It is a dark wood stump
But when I close my eyes with the dead,
It is a splendid magnolia.
The agony of a new bud shoots
Somewhere inside my body.
The splendid glory of the magnolia.

PART II: CHIHA KIM

Whatever

Any
Sound is welcome,
However small.

Lonely
As I am,
I'll not decline
Even a bug-bite
Utter solitude.

At the dead-end of
My thoughts,
Sudden illumination blazes.

My life is not so simple
But is a vast universe,
Where every bug and every sound lives and leaps.

A bitter
Laugh,

And then
A Smile.

I bow with respect
To the withered tree outside,

And a leaf
Falls down like a prayer.

In the Past

All the confusing thoughts from the past
Have disappeared without a trace,

And in that empty space
The shadow of a withered tree lives.

Birds,
Make your nest here!

Sing
New songs not yet heard.
A song of
Barley ripening green
With winter deepening.
A song of plum blossoms
And another of red
Camellias.

Above all, the song of myself,
Not the old self but my self newly-born.

PART II: CHIHA KIM

Heart's Agony

In the spring,
I see
A flower stalk shaking.

The centrifugal power
Pushes itself up
Through the ground,

Forcing the flower to open
And scatter its seeds
In every direction.

The stalk agonizes
And labors.

I shake also.

Tomorrow,
I'll go to the country
To bare myself
And bloom.

New Spring 3

Lonely have I been
All through the winter.

Spring has come blissfully to talk
With the grass
And the new shoots.

It teaches me that loneliness is sheer delusion.
Earth, Air, Water, and Wind
Are my brothers
And my elders in fact.
Their words make me happy again.

A bird's song,
Like a benediction,
Hovers over my head.

PART II: CHIHA KIM

New Spring 4

I am thankful
That I am still alive.

More thankful
That I can enjoy
Three meals a day.

Much more thankful
That I can appreciate
Spring flowers again.

I hold the universe
In my placid heart.

Somewhere under the tree,
I hear the budding sound of life
And a bird's song.

New Spring 6

Bees
Visit flowers,

And children
Play in the park.

These are too much for me
And my heart leaps
At the wonder of all living things.

PART II: CHIHA KIM

New Spring 8

I wonder
How old I really am.

It is three and a half billion years
Since the beginning of life on the earth,
Fifteen billion years
Since the eruption of the cosmos,
And an eternity
Before and after that.

Ah! Eternity

In spite of thousand deaths,
My life is undying.

Now I fear nothing,

And will love
Even a blade of grass
And Me.

The Gaps

In the gaps
Between the apartments,
The cold wind blows, jealous of spring flowers.

Within human bodies
Living in the apartments
Buds also flower.

It is to these gaps that
Spring returns,
Finding even the caged.

Humans are
Gaps

Where new things
Always begin.

PART II: CHIHA KIM

Respect

Heaven rests
On the top of poplars,
And it
Merges into the trees.

You have to climb higher
To appreciate how high a mountain is.

My heart
Leaps joyfully and wildly
At the sight
Of a woman
And children.

The bud of the Cosmos
Shoots everywhere.

Love is
Respect

That spins the world smoothly
By placing others on high.

Love

The flowers have bloomed,
But
No butterflies visit them.

Instead a breathtaking stillness
Pierces my heart.

Cold
And lonely,
I am mad for loving someone,
But
I have no arms
To stretch.

Mad for loving someone,
I wander through the streets
Until my heart and body
Are bone-tired
And bleed inward.

PART II: CHIHA KIM

Flower-envying Cold 1

I await
People in the spring.

To await someone
Feeling the flow of my own blood
Inside me
Is a bitter joy.
And the cosmic dance

Like
Mid-spring snow.

I await
People in the spring.

Flower buds emerge
From empty boughs.

Ilsan Poems 2

I'm alone
In white light.

The river flows
Far in the distance
Where summer clouds pass.

I look
And see death nearby.

Inside the deep
Of my heart,
A wind stirs.

I begin to walk
To meet it.

PART II: CHIHA KIM

Ilsan Poem 4

Crickets
Sing throughout the night.

At their song my heart opens
And embraces the Universe.

Even in the dark, starless sky
I can see green stars

And hear
The sound of the river far away.

This autumn
I may live without longing.

Ilsan Poems 5

The flesh
On my body has departed.

I see only bones.

I dream of a rainbow
Inside these bones
On which the radiant white sun shines.

From the bones
Grass sprouts, and
The sun and moon travel along their marrow.

Day and night
I hear the sound of shamans' songs.

The bones of the city,
The white bones of the streets and
My remnant bones,
All are places
Where a new heaven and earth grows.

PART II: CHIHA KIM

Inner Flesh 1

Mt. Chiak
Is dawning within me,
So I take a walk
Inside myself.
The clean one as well as the dirty one
Walk inside me,
Willingly changing leads,
While a chronic cough follows behind
Along this first snow-covered dusk road.

Inner Flesh 3

When the sun is about to rise,
And the moon is sinking,
Stars are hard to find

Neither the trace of my heart
Nor that of other people is found easily.

In the midst of this vast world,
I think of life.

PART II: CHIHA KIM

Nothing

Out of desire, everything begins.

Out of hunger,
I
Loved you.

This afternoon
When all the insects and worms,
People on the street,
And the sun, moon and clouds are dying,

Love,
Cosmic and unknown,
Shoots out like the wind
From my empty heart.

Its fresh-green
Startles me.

Out of desire
Everything is born.

Loneliness

Lonely
Indeed.

Nothing is left
For me.

I embrace
The sun and moon,

The sick earth,
The lives of dying people,

And the feeble moans
Of the distant forest.

The laughter
Of my family
Is an unexpected gift.

PART II: CHIHA KIM

A Memory

Once I touched her,
I can never forget
Her white skin.

Her skin is gone,
But the white hue still lingers in the air.

It leads me to mountains,
To rivers blazing in the sun
And to fields.

Finally it rests
In my heart

And burns
The night white.

Empty Room

My wife is
Gone.

The empty room
Is full of autumn.

The sky is blue,
And the sun shines brightly.

The murmurs of people
Sound
And fade away,

For the universe today has nested
In my empty heart.

Tonight,
I am ready to die.

Once dead,
I'll rise above the far-off river,
As a crescent moon.

PART II: CHIHA KIM

My Home

How far is it
From the mountaintop to the sun
Where you
Live?

The distance can be measured
Only by my longings.

There at night,
The moon rises over the mountains
Amid my longings.

Beyond the stars
Lies the black hole of Stephen Hawking
And the baby universe.

You are living over there
As humbly as a portulaca.
.
The faraway distance can be measured
Only by my longings.

You, the Cosmos,
Are my home
To which I shall return in the end.

The Sound of Rain

I close my eyes,
And the sound of rain bathes me.

I hear
The rain
that falls from the sky and
Soars on back, after traveling to earth.

With my ears open,
I hear
The breath of all life,

The sighs of far-off trees
that wither under the acid rain,
The early winter rain
that trails a merciless cold.

My ears are wide open
To the sighs of all living things.
The sound of the soaring rain of bitter sighs
And Yongsan shaman's chanting
Reverberate in my mind,
Wide like plantain leaves.

I hear
Its wild cry of
"Man,
What are you doing?!"

PART II: CHIHA KIM

Cricket

At the cricket's song,
A green star

Rests on
My rippling bosom.

All creation in this strange city
On this autumn night
Is clothed in splendor.

Autumn Twilight

Autumn twilight
Is sad to see

After all has gone
Home.

Withered sunflowers
Are traces of summer gone.

The sun blazes red,
Trailing long shadows.

Dusk in the field,
And the moon in my heart.

Tonight I sleep,
Holding the Universe in my heart.

PART II: CHIHA KIM

A New Church

When grass beckons,
And soil and water shout,
I
Go to church
After a long spell.

The church is on a mountain,
Open-walled
And having no roof.

Sun, moon and stars
Pray together here with me.
Comets come and stay,
And the cosmos, across the galaxy and nebulae,
Dances here.

Women bare themselves.
Naked and smiling,
They sing, shaking white handkerchiefs.

Are these allurements?

My
New church.
Church of grass, soil, and water.

CRACKING THE SHELL

New
Society of Jesus.

Am I dreaming?

PART II: CHIHA KIM

Late Autumn

In late Autumn,
Nothing is left
After the leaves are gone.
Only the thunder rumbles
In the empty sky of my heart.

The End of a Day

The evening dusk closes in
as if the last twilight,
consuming itself red,
were exhausted.

The dark river
ebbs full into my heart,

and thousands of moons
rise above my gray hair.

At the end of
a dizzy day,

a new cosmos begins to sprout
in the darkness.

PART II: CHIHA KIM

To the West*

In my heart,
The flame subsides.

In its place a white moon
Rises day and night.

In this cold place
Even twilight fades.

But flowers bloom
In dreams bad,

And past remorse
Now melt into joy.

Heaven rests
On an apricot leaf
Growing between the apartments.

Come now
Beloved,

And
Turn my black life
Into red budding flesh

On my way out
To the West.

* The West here means the Pure Western World of Buddhism, which is similar to Paradise.

Part III: Hyonjong Chong
Zenic Correspondence and Ecological Ecstasy

PART III: HYONJONG CHONG

The Dream of Things 1
—A Tree's Dream

Kissing the sunlight flowing on its leaves,
a tree dreams of Sun's power.
Caressing its cheeks against the rain spattering on its body,
the tree dreams loudly of Rain's blood.
With the green power of the Wind blowing on its boughs,
the tree hears the sound of its own life shaking.

The Island

Among the people is an island,
and there I'd like to be.

PART III: HYONJONG CHONG

Green Joy
—In the Woods in Spring

The sun slides down
in swelling lights
and overflows intoxicated by its own beams.
As the crown of
all that is green and all flowers,
the sun sends smiles to them,
his own crowns.
He smiles worthily
as the father of metaphors
and the spring of green
with the blue breadth of the sky.
The sky is in itself
all joy and a shrine.

Oh, Sun and blue sky
and the green joy of the boughs which,
breathing water floating in the air,
are intoxicated by the sunlight and air
and by their own sap.

The Earth down deep,
rolling its big fragrant eyeballs,
exchanges smiles quietly
with the sun.

Oh! The fragrances
Of beaming earth,

CRACKING THE SHELL

of the sky
and the trees
flow into my funnel-like nose!

PART III: HYONJONG CHONG

A Song in Praise of the Thunder

For the rumbling thunder in summer
that would shake even the bottom of the universe:
How can people wash
their bodies and minds,
clean and cleanse,
and bright and cool
until they become as light as air
and as free as the wind,
until they wear the color of the dawn?

Thunder!
The umbilical cord of your sound
changes us into sweetly smiling newborn babes.
So far nothing on earth
has given us anything comparable to
the clean blood
and the precious food of your sound.
No ideology, no book,
no victory, no ecstasy,
and no argument
can prevent the birth of the new world
where the muscle of your sound annunciates.
It squeezes the bowels of the universe,
and argues the dazzling freedom
of your wayless way.
My petite thunder,
rumbling sporadically inside my brain and ribs,
cannot travel the universe freely like you,

who has no fear of beginning and end.
I want to end this repetition of grave-digging,
take off this smelling skin,
and give a hard blow to the hesitating and
lukewarm movement of my heart.

I want to roll, O Thunder,
up to the height the girl student's yearning eyes measure.
She, whose eyes resemble grapes tinged with bluish powder,
foiled me yesterday by asking,
"Professor, how are you doing nowadays?"
in a shy voice, as if she feared that the floating flower seeds,
surprised by her voice, would take root in a hill.

O always perilous truth,
naked body fighting against death!
My alchemy burns within the poems
while my body aches.
O Thunder! Become the keynote
of my life and song, though impure as fried rice.
O you who lead us to nirvana
by roaring away our miserable agonies.

Even the echoes of your sound
are already immanent in your roaring.
Look! Your newborn babe, a bare-naked one,
takes your clean blood and your precious food.
It even marvels at your dazzling wayward ways.
T-H-U-N-D-E-R-I-N-G!

PART III: HYONJONG CHONG

Poetry Writing Class

Though my words are good sometimes,
what is better
is listening to the live, green words
either of budding flowers or of dying people.
Running at full speed is better than
listening to accustomed words.
Falling and bleeding while running
is better still.
The word "perspective" may, for example,
bring to mind the image of a boundless landscape,
but what is better is to climb a tree
and to look down upon the world from above.
Why don't you go to the river,
catch a live fish
and hold it firmly between your palms,
rather than listening to my stammering words?
Fresh confusion is better indeed,
so go raid a melon patch in the dead of night.
Catch a sleeping bird and hold it in your hand
and feel its throbbing heart and warm body
on your palm.
This is the depth of the world!
Therefore, rather than looking up at your teacher's face,
it's better to kiss your lover's lips
and melt into the action.
Having looked up at the blue sky once,
become the blueness or the air of autonomy,
shake apart the classroom windows

and furl yourself into the vast sky wide and blue!
Anyway, be a useless man,
though you have a human shape.
Chuang Tzu talked about
the usefulness of the useless.
At least walk in the gait of
the useless endeavor.

You are yourself and no one else,
and you are everyone.
The inevitable beginning of love,
the inevitable beginning of sorrow,
and the beginning of all toppling laughter.
Let the flower, blood, tree, melon, fish, bird, lover
and the blue sky you touched
bloom in your flesh and swim in your blood.
Day and night unfurl yourself on the world like the blue sky
that your bruised body and aspiring breath
begot with love.

PART III: HYONJONG CHONG

An Elementary School in the Country

Oh, an elementary school in the country,
its view embraces me in its bosom.
In its bosom
I am embraced
again and again.

In all the world,
the following only exist *there*:

holy peace,
flowers of time,
dreaming echoes,
obstinate purity,
convergence of cosmic holiness.

Though you condense all the haze from the forests of the world
into a bean-size pill,
it cannot rival the high density
of the children's breathes, those of the living universes.
However hard you may try,
how can your cheek touch
the young breath of the air *there*
with your mere words?

Ah, an elementary school in the country!

The Haze of Life

Though I sing for all my life,
can my song even stand beside a pheasant's song
that sounds occasionally from that mountain,
and plunges me suddenly into the bottomless sea of life?
Can my song be compared
to the pheasant's husky sound
as if his throat were almost full of
worms, dust and shadows?
To the pheasant's inhumanized song
that ignores any singing technique and overflows because of
    the exuberance of his own life?

My song breathes
the haze of life,
rising up from all creation.
I wish my words were
the haze of life.

PART III: HYONJONG CHONG

To My Nature

Holding a more delicious-looking grass,
I seduce a goat grazing on other grass.
It's for no other reason than
to look into his eyes closely
and touch him.
Through his eyes
and through the sense of touching his coat,
I return to my own nature.
What exuberance overflows the leaves!
Animals draw me to them
so helplessly.
I come to return to my nature
unaware.

What exuberance overflows the levees!

A Good Landscape

On a snowy day in late winter,
when the temperature was warm and the snow mellow,
a man and a woman's footsteps disappeared into the woods.
They were covered with snow, resembling a babe's bottom.

Because they did *that act* leaning against the chestnut tree,
blowing their thick winter breaths into the valley,
this year's spring has come earlier than usual.
The chestnut tree, bewildered, has opened all its flowers
in just half a day, instead of taking several days, as usual.

PART III: HYONJONG CHONG

The Mystery of the Path

If I look at you, O Path, you disappear
somewhere(!) over the valley.
Circling around the waist of a low hill,
you make me breathless and absorb me
endlessly.
Turning around the hill's waist
and over
the valley,
you disappear into the
unknown.
Your sight
stimulates me unrestrainably.
My body burns red,
my heart palpitates,
and my bowels itch.
Oh Path, you are
an exposed mystery,
an umbilical cord connecting
to numerous curious worlds.
Beyond you a new village
is born.
You lead us into open spaces,
hidden breathes
and glistening faces.
Circling around the mountain's waist
and passing over the valley resembling a woman's loin,
you are always in heat.
You are indeed my libido.

CRACKING THE SHELL

Over the path it disappears(!),
and there appears at last
our spring of longing,
root of desire
and jeweled island of adventure.

My sighs travel farther and farther.
Oh Path,
you are an exposed mystery.

PART III: HYONJONG CHONG

After Being Stung by a Bee

Really excited,
I picked apples for the first time
on a ladder.

The best ripened one on the top branch
reached unmistakably for my hand.
Upon grabbing the apple—
ooh, a pain greeted my finger.
I'd been stung. (The bee was hidden within the crevice of the
 overly ripened apple.)
The pain in my finger
was getting worse as time passed.
(It would be too easy to merely take away
a cautionary lesson from this incident.)
Though I was at ends with my ailing finger,
my mind, on the other hand, overflowed abundantly
like apple trees in Autumn.
Even pain is a way of colluding with Creation.
Riding the infinitesimal poison,
I mixed my body
with the vast depth of nature.

The Field Is Desolate

With the Autumn sun and air,
and the ripening rice,
Everything is glittering!

But
alas, the field is desolate.
All the grasshoppers are gone...

Oh, this ominous silence.
The golden chain of life is broken.

PART III: HYONJONG CHONG

In a Spoonful of Earth

They say there are 150 million microorganisms
in a spoonful of earth.

Why not? The enormous universe is living
within that spoonful of earth.

As I was walking along dirt roads,
stepping on ants at times,
I would feel amazing pressure
on the soles of my feet.
Now I see the pressure was,
in reality, the force of a billion
microorganisms thrusting upward!

A Flower

While in the corridor,
I noticed a woman's breathtakingly
beautiful legs. As I was climbing down the slope,
wholly absorbed in this thought,
a colleague of mine, heading in the opposite direction,
said to me in a muscular voice of certainty,
"You must be overtaken by the Muse!"
I smiled as I passed him
and fell again into my thought.
"Hmm, what a sharp mind-reader!"
The glittering of flesh is
a walking window opening into the primitive—our home.
I imagined a flower (poetry) of raw flesh,
which the vortex of energy heated
in the bellow finally made it bloom.

PART III: HYONJONG CHONG

How Bright It Is!

It is bright
with the persimmons on the tree.
With the red persimmons
glowing like red bulbs,
the whole world is bright.
Even if this sunlight
and that sunlight were combined,
it wouldn't be as bright as those red bulbs.
Though frost falls and winter comes,
I won't pick them; I'll leave them alone.
How abundant it is!
The whole universe is full,
and the magpies and crows are fully fed also.
My mind races over there
into the persimmons
and glows brightly on the bough.

A Song in Praise of Bark

Barks of
living trees!
Whenever I look at you,
I want to feel you
and touch you with my palm.
A mere touch channels
my body temperature and yours
and connects our breathes together.
All of a sudden your sap
rises within my body.
What is it that you,
having endured long and hard,
are wrapping within?
Years and ages,
(I wonder what threw stones into you
that your growth rings circle?)
blood and flesh,
sun and wind,
breath,
bird's dream,
animal's refuge and desire
insect's ——
antennae and eyes, and
loneliness,
the sound of rivulets,
the secrets of flowers,
the warmth
and deep night.

PART III: HYONJONG CHONG

All these are enclosed
within your bark,
thunder and starlight
stones and flames
also.

In the Spring

At the azalea's flame
I also
burn.
I burn out
even into ashes
at this flame.
An epileptic fit seems to seize me
when I look at the shooting buds.
It's worthwhile even to expire
under the cherry blossoms.
Breathlessly blooming flowers and new buds!
Any deviations are acceptable
under your violence.

PART III: HYONJONG CHONG

That Bouquet

On my way back from the summit of Mt. Macchu Picchu,
our train stopped for a while
for unknown reasons.
I got off the train.
An Inca girl of
four or five years old
(Could such a small human being exist!)
was standing there, holding a bouquet
at twilight.
She was standing there as if she were part of the landscape,
holding a bouquet
in that unbearable dusk of twilight,
when you can always hear the breathing sound of seeds.
I approached her.
Through the veil of dusk I saw
her almost invisible smile.
At such times our eyes are a universe.
The earth shines with the gem of such smiles,
and streams flow in the innocence of these smiles.
Her smile spread farther and farther
in the brightness of dusk.
I asked how much it was for the bouquet,
then paid 2 *sols* and received it.
My empty heart expanded boundlessly.

The Deep Earth

When the trail on the hill was a dust lane,
it was really deep.
After it was paved,
the depth disappeared from the road.

The nymphs in the woods also departed.

Deep earth
and shallow asphalt.

Animal-like convenience
and man-like inconvenience.

Profound nature
and superficial culture.

PART III: HYONJONG CHONG

A Summer Day

The leisure hours on a summer day, when
the thunder is rolling about within the clouds,
the rain starts and stops at intervals,
and the cuckoos' singing is heard
on such summer afternoons.
I am blessed with grace
indeed in those hours.

Though the leisure hours, thunder, rain
and the sound of cuckoos are treasures,
their concert makes me suffer from euphoria.
They harmonize me into one body
with the leisure hour,
the thunder,
the rain
and the sound of cuckoos.
Then I overflow the universe.

The soft and circular sounds
of cars and
sirens break the treasures
contemptibly,
their echoes reverberating in my body,
the grace of one summer day.

The Dew

Look at the river, our blood.
Look at the wind, our breath.
Look at the earth, our flesh.

Look at the clouds, our philosophy.
Look at the trees, our poems.
Look at the birds, our dreams.

Oh, look at the insects, our loneliness.
Look at the horizon, our longing.
Look at the flowers of *samadhi*, our joy.

Where are you going? Into whose body?
With your throbbing heart, into whose breath?
The way opens, the infinite way of...

Trees beget clouds beget
Rivers beget birds beget
wind and wind
begets trees...

The cool and blue way opens and
I am intoxicated and dizzy at the way's urging,
the breath's flow, the water's flow, and the blood's flow.

The big cobweb on that pathway,
and the drop of dew ripened on it.
True Void leads to Delicate Creation

PART III: HYONJONG CHONG

The dew that swallowed the sun;
The dew that the wind of all creation rolled into being;
The dew that ate the thunder of all creation roasted;
The dew that squeezed all creation into a drop of juice;
The dew that slept with the thunder and became pregnant;
The dew that mirrored Neptune and Pluto;
The dew that at last formed on a leaf
rolled by the voice of birds
after having traveled through the bowels of worms.

That Curved Line

I love exceedingly
the curved lines
of the cows and horses
grazing in the field.

The lines,
the image of life.
The lines,
the bonanza of peace.

Why is it so unbearably
good,
that curved line?

PART III: HYONJONG CHONG

That Toad

In the white pine forests of Mt. Chukrong,
I came across, after a long absence,
a brown toad crouching on the mossy stone.
Though I crouched near to watch him, he did not move at all
whether in peacefulness or in hiding.
An elusive creature with its back as deep and thick as nature
    God made.
The forest's shadow, the smell of the earth and the sound of
    the brook
rested on his dark brown back.
All insects, grass sky
and even the infinite celestial bodies
were vivid against the dark color of his back.

Riding on his back today,
I recover myself a little.

Trees of the World

I wonder what kinds of works
trees of the world are doing?
They willingly take root in the soil of the man
who enjoys watching them.

Day after day he watches them and loves them more
until his heart pounds wild and blue at their beauty.
They push up saps in every corner of the body
and channel their saps higher and higher up to the sky.
They are springs of perfect-round tension!

Trees! Don't you hear day after day
the ever expanding, throbbing energy of first love
full in the sky, on the earth and in our hearts?

PART III: HYONJONG CHONG

A God

Elzieard Bouffier, tree-planter.
A godly man made known to me by a French writer.
A country dweller who knew no letters,
but who revived the dead land and made it teem with creatures
by planting trees in the deserted highlands of the Alps
and by supplying water and by calling in the birds.
He is a god, totally indifferent to worldly affairs.
He's silent
and, above all else, without using such things as words,
he talks only with the language
of planted trees,
flowing water,
chirping birds and
blooming flowers.
He is a god
made in man's image.

The Sound of Birds

Look at the sound of the skylark.
The overflowing words are
"build your house here,
build your house here."
Also the sound of the cuckoo:
"build your house here,
build your house here."
Some mountain birds also say,
"build your house here…"

Thus the infinity of this sound
opens and opens wider still
so that I can see the universe of
wind, shadows and green,
the universe of soil and insects,
and thunder and lightening…

When spring comes I always live
in the house of the sound of birds.
It is endlessly round, wide
and comfortable.

PART III: HYONJONG CHONG

My Pleasing Stimulants

My pleasing stimulants are
thunder and lightening,
birds of the world,
trees of the earth,
flowers and grass,
pretty women,
full moons about to burst,
shudder! insects and
those terrible animals.
How sacred
are
my throat and
hardly bearable, beggarly things in any respect?
I—beggar (sticking to the system),
system—beggar (despairing at the system which does not
 accept exceptions),
custom—comfortable despair (oh, the myth of wings).
The system would be O.K. if it were silky-smooth and soft
 enough
to arouse you at mere touch.
But this is a "marvelous" fried rice of millet, despair and
 comedy,
so unbelievably delicious
that I eat it again and again
until my drowned body floats down in the honey sea of nausea.
Agonizing hearts, don't feign purposelessly.
Unpleasant stimulants, do you want me to love you,
Rather pity me and forgive me?

CRACKING THE SHELL

Well, my heart wanders endlessly elsewhere,
and so I will trust my body to my pleasing stimulants.
Thunder and lightening,
birds of the world,
trees of the earth,
flowers and grass,
pretty women,
full moons about to burst,
shudder! insects,
those terrible animals and
your
fragrant breath.

PART III: HYONJONG CHONG

Flower Petals

I walk along the road,
strewn with fallen cherry blossoms.
In reality, I am not walking but floating instead.
Whoops! I am floating,
my mind is dazzled;
I am leaving the ground soaring.
The sky is spread upon the earth
with flower petals,
and the earth is already afloat.
O the flower petals that make the earth float!
Is this a dream?
Flower petals are falling,
and the earth is soaring.
With every falling petal,
the earth soars fluttering.
Is this a dream?
Oooh, flower petals!

My Blood Glittering in the Sky at Night

Stars, are you glittering?
I am glittering also.
We are brothers sharing calcium and iron.
The thought that we are far apart
and, therefore, separate beings is an illusion.
This mere body, comprising three worlds and a cosmos,
is a unified spiritual being even death cannot kill.

That's the reason we count stars and men by turns,
like one star, one man and two stars, two men.
Therefore, isn't this legend true?
Aren't we ourselves legends,
the legend of calcium
and that of iron?

My bones glitter in the sky at night.
My blood glitters in the sky at night.

PART III: HYONJONG CHONG

The Seeds of Clouds

Emiliana Huxleyi, a vegetable plankton living in the sea, is one
　　of the most essential parts of the biosphere, having excel-
　　lent power for absorbing carbon dioxide and yielding me-
　　thyl sulfide, the seeds of clouds.

Emiliana Huxleyi,
the seeds and womb
of clouds!
Don't kill
Miss Emiliana please.
She looks like a ball wrought with wool
and has many crater-like holes.
If Miss Emiliana dies
from the contaminated sea,
there will be no clouds and no rain.

It wasn't accidental
that I've been singing about the clouds,
and our flesh and blood,
though I didn't know much about
biology, meteorology,
sea physics or earth chemistry.
In reality, clouds are the seed of our flesh
and that of our blood, aren't they?

The living things of earth
and our bodies change
from gas into solid,

and then into liquid in turns.
Aren't we plankton, too,
in bottomless, endless time?
Aren't we grass
and clouds also?

As there wouldn't be clouds without Miss Emiliana,
would we exist without clouds?
Please don't kill the clouds.
A dead cloud is our death.
A dead cloud is dead sky.
A dead sky is dead earth.

About the Translator

Won-Chung Kim is Professor of English Literature at Sungkyunkwan University in Seoul, Korea. He earned his Ph.D. in English poetry at the University of Iowa in 1993. His main areas of research are contemporary American poetry, ecological literature and translation. He has translated the works of Chiha Kim (*Heart's Agony*, White Pine Press, 1998), Seungho Choi (*Flowers in the Toilet Bowl*, Homa & Sekey Books, 2004), Jl-woo Hwang (*Even Birds Leave the World*, White Pine Press, 2005, *Because of the Rain: Korean Zen Poems*, White Pine Press, 2005), and Shin Kyungrim (*A Love Song for the Earnest: Selected Poems of Shin Kyungrim*, Homa & Sekey Books, 2006).

Homa & Sekey Books Titles on Korea (1)

East and West: Fusion of Horizons
By Kwang-Sae Lee, Kent State University
ISBN 1931907269, Order No 1030, 6 x 9, Hardcover, $59.95, £35.00
ISBN 1931907331, Order No 1041, 6 x 9, Paperback, $34.95, £22.00
Philosophy/Culture/Comparative Studies, 2006, xii, 522pp

A Topography of Confucian Discourse: Politico-philosophical Reflections on Confucian Discourse since Modernity
By Lee Seung-hwan, Korea University
ISBN 1931907277, Order No 1031, 6 x 9, Hardcover, $49.95, £30.00
ISBN 193190734X, Order No 1042, 6 x 9, Paperback, $29.95, £19.00
History/Culture/Philosophy, 2006, xii, 260pp

Developmental Dictatorship and the Park Chung-hee Era: The Shaping of Modernity in the Republic of Korea
Edited by Lee Byeong-cheon, Kangwon National University
ISBN 1931907285, Order No 1032, 6 x 9, Hardcover, $54.95, £32.00
ISBN 1931907358, Order No 1043, 6 x 9, Paperback, $32.95, £20.00
History/Politics, 2006, xviii, 384pp

The Gwangju Uprising: The Pivotal Democratic Movement That Changed the History of Modern Korea
By Choi Jungwoon, Seoul National University
ISBN 1931907293, Order No 1033, 6 x 9, Hardcover, $49.95, £31.00
ISBN 1931907366, Order No 1044, 6 x 9, Paperback, $29.95, £19.00
History/Politics, 2006, xx, 326pp

**The Land of Scholars:
Two Thousand Years of Korean Confucianism**
By Kang Jae-eun
ISBN 1931907307, Order No 1034, 6 x 9, Hardcover, $59.95, £35.00
ISBN 1931907374, Order No 1045, 6 x 9, Paperback, $34.95, £22.00
History/Culture/Philosophy, 2006, xxx, 516pp

Korea's Pastimes and Customs: A Social History
By Lee E-Wha. 16 pages of color photos. B&W illustrations throughout.
ISBN 1931907382, Order No 1035, 6 x 9, Paperback, $29.95, £21.00
History/Culture, 2006, x, 264pp

Homa & Sekey Books Titles on Korea (2)

A Love Song for the Earnest: Selected Poems of Shin Kyungrim
ISBN: 1931907390, Order No 1037, 5 ½ x 8 ½, Paperback, xxiv, 72pp
Poetry, $11.95, 2006

Cracking the Shell: Three Korean Ecopoets
By Seungho Choi, Chiha Kim, and Hyonjong Chong
ISBN: 1931907404, Order No 1038, 5 ½ x 8 ½, Paperback, xxviii, 108pp
Poetry, $12.95, 2006

Sunrise over the East Sea: Selected Poems of Park Hi-jin
ISBN: 1931907412, Order No 1039, 5 ½ x 8 ½, Paperback, xiv, 124pp
Poetry, $10.95, 2006

Fragrance of Poetry: Korean-American Literature.
Ed. by Yearn Hong Choi, Ph.D., 5 ½ x 8 ½, Paperback, 108pp
ISBN: 1931907226, Order No. 1027, **Poetry**, $13.95, 2005

A Floating City on the Water: A Novel by Jang-Soon Sohn
ISBN: 1931907188, Order No: 1025, 5½ x 8½, Paperback, 178pp
Fiction, $14.95, 2005

Korean Drama Under Japanese Occupation:
Plays by Ch'i-jin Yu & Man-sik Ch'ae, 5½ x 8½, Paperback, x, 178pp
ISBN: 193190717X, Order No: 1026, **Drama**, $16.95, 2004

The Curse of Kim's Daughters: A Novel By Park Kyong-ni
ISBN: 1931907102, Order No: 1018, 5½ x 8½, Paperback, 299pp
Fiction, $18.95, 2004

I Want to Hijack an Airplane: Selected Poems of Kim Seung-Hee
ISBN: 1931907137, Order No: 1021, 5½ x 8½, Paperback, xiv, 188pp
Poetry, $15.95, 2004

Flowers in the Toilet Bowl: Selected Poems of Choi Seungho
ISBN: 1931907110, Order No: 1022, 5½ x 8½, Paperback, xxvi, 73pp
Poetry, $12.95, 2004

Drawing Lines: Selected Poems of Moon Dok-su
ISBN: 1931907129, Order No: 1023, 5½ x 8½, Paperback, xvi, 82pp
Poetry, $11.95, 2004

Homa & Sekey Books Titles on Korea (3)

What the Spider Said: Poems of Chang Soo Ko
ISBN: 1931907145, Order No: 1024, 5½ x 8½
Paperback, xii, 74pp, **Poetry,** $10.95, 2004

Surfacing Sadness:
A Centennial of Korean-American Literature 1903-2003
Ed. by Yearn Hong Choi, Ph.D & Haeng Ja Kim
ISBN: 1931907099, Order No: 1017, 6 x 9, Hardcover, xxvi,
216pp, **Asian-American Studies/Literature,** $25.00, 2003

Father and Son: A Novel by Han Sung-won,
ISBN: 1931907048, Order No: 1010, 5½ x 8½, Paperback, 285pp,
2002, **Fiction,** $17.95

Reflections on a Mask: Two Novellas by Ch'oe In-hun.
ISBN: 1931907056, Order No: 1011, 5½ x 8½, Paperback, 258pp,
2002, **Fiction,** $16.95

Unspoken Voices: Selected Short Stories by Korean Women Writers By Park Kyong-ni, et al.
ISBN: 1931907064, Order No: 1012, 5½ x 8½, Paperback, 266pp,
2002, **Fiction,** $16.95

The General's Beard: Two Novellas by Lee Oyoung,
ISBN: 1931907072, Order No: 1013, 5½ x 8½, Paperback, 182pp,
2002, **Fiction,** $14.95

Farmers: A Novel by Lee Mu-young,
ISBN: 1931907080, Order No: 1014, 5½ x 8½, Paperback, 216pp,
2002, **Fiction,** $15.95

www.homabooks.com

Ordering Information: Within U.S.: $5.00 for the first item, $1.50 for each additional item. **Outside U.S.:** $10.00 for the first item, $5.00 for each additional item. All major credit cards accepted. You may also send a check or money order in U.S. fund (payable to Homa & Sekey Books) to: Orders Department, Homa & Sekey Books, P. O. Box 103, Dumont, NJ 07628 U.S.A. Tel: 800-870-HOMA, 201-261-8810; Fax: 201-261-8890, 201-384-6055; Email: info@homabooks.com